In Real Life
Exploring tough questions facing youth today

WHO IS GOD?
Engaging the Mystery

ISBN 978-1-949628-20-3
Printed in the United States of America.
10 9 8 7 6 5 4 3 2 1   22 21 20 19

Published by The Pastoral Center, http://pastoral.center.

Developed in partnership with MennoMedia and Brethren Press. Series editors: Fumiaki Tosu, Ann Naffziger, and Paul Canavese. *Who Is God?: Engaging the Mystery:* Writer, Tracy Wenger Sadd. Project editor, Lani Wright. Staff editors, Susan E. Janzen, Julie Garber, and James Deaton. Updated design, Paul Stocksdale.

All rights reserved. Purchase of this book includes a license to reproduce this resource for use in a single parish, school, or other similar organization. You are allowed to share and make unlimited copies only for use within the organization that licensed it. If you serve more than one organization, each should purchase its own license. You may not post this document to any web site without explicit permission to do so. Outside of these conditions, no part of this book may be reproduced in any form or by any means, electronic or mechanical, including photocopying, recording, taping, or via any retrieval system, without the written permission of The Pastoral Center, 1212 Versailles Ave., Alameda, CA 94501. Thank you for cooperating with our honor system regarding our licenses.

For questions or to order additional copies or licenses, please call 1-844-727-8672 or visit http://pastoral.center.

Portions of this work © 2019 by The Pastoral Center / PastoralCenter.com. Adapted and published with permission from Generation Why Bible Studies. © 1997, 2015 Brethren Press, Elgin, IL 60120 and MennoMedia, Harrisonburg, VA 22803, U.S.A. All rights reserved.

Unless otherwise noted, the Scripture passages contained herein are from the *New Revised Standard Version of the Bible*, copyright © 1989 by the National Council of the Churches of Christ in the United States of America. Used by permission. All rights reserved.

» OVERVIEW

When conversing online, the acronym IRL stands for "in real life." The virtual world of social media, text chats, blogs, and more have the power to remove us from the real world. What we experience online can skew our perspective on what it means to be human. It can numb us, incite us, distract us, depress us, confuse us, and make us rude or impatient. Strangely, this supposedly "social" and "connected" technology can profoundly disconnect us from others.

Religious faith can also place us in a bubble, especially when it distances us from others. When we keep the prophetic message at a safe distance, obscured in theological language and abstractions, we are missing the whole point. And when we see our parish as an insider club that serves itself, we can forget the radically inclusive message entrusted to us: God's love is for *everyone*, and God expects us to transform the *whole world* through that love.

Through the incarnation, God showed up in the real world to show us that our faith is not just about talking the talk, but also walking the walk. It can be risky. It can be confusing. It can hurt. But living out our faith can also bring us great purpose, peace, and joy.

This series connects the Bible with the tough questions that youth (and adults) encounter in their neighborhood, in school, among friends, and even online. This process will help you as a leader break open these issues in a fun and meaningful way, sparking conversation and the kind of life change Jesus invites us to embrace.

» THE ROLE OF PARENTS

As children enter middle school and high school, they become more independent, self-reliant, and, well, self-centered. This can bring parents to make assumptions that this is the time to step back, giving their child more space to form their identity. While there is truth to that at some level (adolescents definitely shouldn't be smothered), this is a stage of life when parents should in fact *lean in*. The apparent confidence and bluster youth show on the outside can mask the insecurity and confusion on the inside. Youth need their parents to be involved more than ever.

» WHOLE FAMILY FORMATION

Parents are the primary teachers of their own children, and parishes are waking up to the fact that faith formation programs need to bring parents into the process if they hope to see faith passed on to the next generation. Recent studies give us more and more evidence that the role of parents is the most important factor in determining whether a child will embrace faith as they move toward adulthood. Research from the Center for the Applied Research on the Apostolate shows that parents who talk about their faith and show through their actions that their faith is important to them are more likely to have children who remain Catholic.

More about Whole Family Formation >>>>

To learn more about how your parish can take a comprehensive whole family approach to faith formation, visit **GrowingUpCatholic.com**.

While whole family events with elementary-aged children are on the rise, the role of parents can be an afterthought in youth ministry. We have designed the sessions in this series to work with or without parents present, and we encourage you to offer them as parent-child events.

If you choose to involve parents, it is important to consider before each session how to best do so. Many of the activities in this series are high-energy, creative, or silly. Some parents may need some encouragement to get out of their heads and have fun with the group. A few activities involving physical contact would be inappropriate for parents and youth to participate together, and we have noted them as such.

There are a number of ways to approach discussions with parent participation. Unless you have a small group, you will likely want to break into smaller groups for conversation. Some youth may be self-conscious and unable to be completely honest and open in a group situation with a parent present. For this reason, you may choose in some cases to assign parents to different groups from their own children, or to have separate parent and child groups altogether. Be sure to cover expectations around confidentiality. It is inappropriate for a parent (or youth) to share with another parent what their child said in a small group.

Note that even if parents and their children do not share all conversations together in the session, they will still have a valuable shared experience and can have extended conversations about it later.

>> **THANK YOU**

The role you play in gathering, animating, praying with, and forming youth is a valuable one. Thank you for all you do to serve the church and its families!

Bible-based Explorations of Issues Facing Youth

WHO IS GOD?
Engaging the Mystery

>> INTRODUCTION

To discover someone's identity—to get to the essence, beyond the basics of name, age, occupation, and a few hobbies—is a complex and difficult task. When God is the "someone" whose identity is sought, the task is quite impossible. Moses had a difficult time even finding out what God wanted to be called. In Exodus 3, when Moses asked after God's name, God responded cryptically, "I AM WHO I AM" (or "I WILL BE WHAT I WILL BE").

Where can we find clues about who God is? God is, essentially, indescribable—beyond space, beyond time, beyond human comprehension. Yet God desires to be known and to relate to humanity. These sessions focus on a few of the ways we glimpse the character of the divine: in what God created, in the biblical record of God's faithfulness, through the psalmist's witness, in the images and metaphors the biblical writers use, and through church tradition.

It is tempting to want full knowledge and absolute certainty. When leading the sessions, remember that no one can or should know everything about God. Pray for wisdom in responding to questions participants will ask—questions that have no answers, or at least no easy answers. It is impossible to hand anyone a comprehensive understanding of God. But it *is* possible to invite participants to explore how the Bible and church tradition witness to how humans have wrestled with trying to know God. It *is* possible to help participants understand the complexity and difficulty in trying to answer questions about God. It *is* possible to encourage participants to get to know God, by inviting them to experience God's presence and to wrestle with the Mystery in their own lives.

Preparation Alert >>>>

Sessions 1, 3, and 5 suggest as an option contacting people or groups ahead of time to do specific tasks. In Session 2, there is an option of planting a tree for a future generation. You may need to order a seedling ahead of time and get permission to plant it somewhere on the church property.

God is, essentially, indescribable–beyond space, beyond time, beyond human comprehension. Yet God desires to be known and to relate to humanity. Yet we glimpse the character of the divine in what God created, in the biblical record of God's faithfulness, through the psalmist's witness, in the images and metaphors the biblical writers use, and through church tradition.

In Real Life | Who Is God?

EXTENDER SESSION

Extender sessions suggest special activities related to the issue of the unit. They help accommodate the diversity of parish schedules. Since each unit is undated, participants may study units in their entirety and still participate in special events of the parish that get scheduled simultaneously with youth group time. Extender sessions can be used anytime, but the one for this unit best follows **Session 5**. Calculate now whether or not you will be using the extender session.

THE TEACHING PLAN: The parts of the session guide

- **Faith story.** The session is rooted in this Bible passage.
- **Faith focus.** The story of the passage in a nutshell.
- **Session goal.** The entire session is built around this goal. What changes—in knowledge, attitude, and/or action—do you desire in your group?
- **Materials needed and advance preparation.** This is what you will need if the session is to go smoothly. You'll feel more at ease if you've taken care of these details before you meet your group.

FROM LIFE TO BIBLE TO LIFE

The session plan is called *life-centered*. However, when we write each session, we always begin with scripture. We ask, what does this particular passage say, especially to youth? Each session moves from life to Bible to life. So the Bible is really at the center of this way of teaching.

In every session we try to hit upon a tough question that participants might ask. Find out what questions on this issue are important for *your* group. By all means, bring your own input and invite your group members to add their own experiences.

TEACHING THE SESSION

The five step-by-step movements will carry you from *life to the Bible and back to life*. Each session takes about 45 to 50 minutes. If there is a handout sheet for the session, take note of any complementary activities and stories.

1. **Focus.** Intended to create a friendly climate within the group and to *draw attention* to the issue.
2. **Connect.** Invites participants to *express* their own life experience about the issue, through talking, drawing, role playing, and other activities. Also uses memory, reason, or imagination to get the group thinking about *why* they view the issue the way they do.
3. **Explore the Bible.** What does the Bible *say* about the issue? With a minimum of lecturing, dig into the faith story and search for answers to questions raised in the first activities. The Insights from Scripture section will help clarify the faith story. Help participants discover how the faith community understands the Bible passage.
4. **Apply** the faith story. What does the Bible passage *mean* for contemporary life? This is the "aha!" moment when participants realize the faith story has wisdom for *their* lives.
5. **Respond.** Why does the Bible passage *matter*? What will the group do about the issue in light of what they have learned from their own experiences set alongside the faith story? How can we *live* the faith story rather than pass it off as a mere intellectual exercise?

LOOK AHEAD

Here are reminders for what you need to do for the next session or two.

INSIGHTS FROM SCRIPTURE

Here is a resource for Explore the Bible. Don't try to use all the material given. Take what you need to lead the session and answer questions your group may have. Let the Insights section inspire you to think and study more about the passage for the session.

›› HANDOUT SHEETS

Occasionally, there will be a handout sheet to complement your session. If you choose to use this, make enough copies for the group in advance of the session. These sheets may include questions, stories, agree/disagree exercises, charts, pictures, and other materials to stimulate thinking and discussion.

Generally, no participant preparation is required unless the session plan calls for you to contact selected group members for specific tasks.

Exploring tough questions facing youth today

>>> **SESSION 1**

GOD CREATES >>>

>> KEY VERSES

For what can be known about God is plain to them, because God has shown it to them. Ever since the creation of the world [the] eternal power and divine nature, invisible though they are, have been understood and seen through the things [the Creator] has made. (Romans 1:19-20a)

>> FAITH STORY

Romans 1:19-20a; Psalm 104:10-32

>> FAITH FOCUS

In this passage, Paul admonished the Romans for denying knowledge of God while at the same time saying they had seen and experienced the wonder of nature. According to Paul, if the Romans had seen the world God created, they had also seen God, the Creator. What can be known about God, in addition to divine revelation to Israel, through the Bible, and in Jesus Christ, can be known by looking at what the Creator made. At the very least, creation reveals that God is loving, awesome, beautiful, and powerful.

>> SESSION GOAL

In a culture that is sometimes suspicious of the relationship between nature and God, invite participants to clarify what we can discover about God in creation, as well as what creation cannot tell us about God.

TEACHING PLAN

1. FOCUS 5-15 minutes

>> **Option A:** Give out paper and markers. Tell participants they will have about 10 minutes to draw or sketch one of their favorite places in nature. Emphasize that it need not be an artistic drawing, but simply a sketch. Markers may help. Allow people to converse as they draw. Some will be faster than others. Allow time to come to a point where they think they are finished. Go to Connect, **Option A**.

>> **Option B:** Divide the group into pairs. Give out index cards and pencils. Tell participants they will have about 10 minutes to write a three-sentence biography of God. Go to Connect, **Option B**.

>> **Materials needed and advance preparation**

- Unlined paper and markers (*Option A*, Focus)
- Index cards and pencils (*Option B and C*, Focus)
- Copies of the handout sheet for Session 1
- Bibles
- Writing paper and pencils; chalkboard/chalk or newsprint/markers
- Team prize for memory game (Variation in Explore the Bible)
- Pick an outside location to meet after participants find things not human made (*Option A and B*, Apply).
- Basket or box (*Option C*, Apply)
- Invite a church leader to spend time with the group, exploring questions about God (*Option C*, Apply).
- Song books, words to songs, instruments (*Option D*, Respond)

> "...[E]very creature can be called a theophany. It is the manifestation of the hidden... the visibility of the invisible. This is not to say that what is shown in a creature is the essence of God, for God is essentially unknowable. Rather, what is manifested is an expression of God's essence... the soul of every creature is derived from the one Soul. God therefore, is not simply in every creature, but is the essence of every creature. At heart, creation—including our creatureliness—is a showing forth of the mystery of God."

John Scotus Eriugena, 9th-century Scottish teacher, summarized by J. Philip Newell in *The Book of Creation*

>> **Option C:** Give out index cards and pencils. To introduce the topic "Who is God?" invite participants to write any question(s) they have about God on an index card. They do not need to write their names. Collect the questions for later use. Go to Connect, **Option C**.

2. CONNECT 5-10 minutes

>> **Option A:** Invite sharing in pairs, small groups, or in the entire group what they like about the place they drew.

>> **Option B:** Stay in pairs, and make a list on the back of the index card of every source they can think of from which they get information about God. (If people have trouble with this, remind them to consider where they got the information used in the biography from Focus.)

>> **Option C:** Have participants pair up. On the back of one of the index cards, direct the pairs to list every source they know from which the group might find information to answer the questions they wrote about God.

3. EXPLORE THE BIBLE 15-20 minutes

Shift to this activity by saying: *The Bible suggests that we can find out about God by studying and experiencing what God made. Let's consider what this is...*

Distribute the handout sheets. Working as individuals or in small groups, have people listen for all the things God made, as you read Psalm 104:10-32 (read slowly, and meditatively, repeating phrases that speak to you). Tell them that after you read the psalm, each group will have 5 minutes to write down as many things as they can remember named in the psalm that were created by God.

Have one group write all the things they remembered on the chalkboard or newsprint. Have a second group add ones they remembered that the first group did not (sort of like the games Boggle or Scattergories). Continue this way until all groups have shared. You as leader should add any items that are still missing. Invite additions that group members have experienced.

Variation: Get participants to listen to this long psalm by turning the above activity into a competition between two teams (boys vs. girls; curly hair vs straight; other combinations). Offer a prize to the team that remembered the most created things.

Here is a nearly comprehensive list of created things named in Psalm 104:10-32. Read over it ahead of time, since you may want to add or subtract things:

springs	human heart	water	Leviathan
people	young lions	wild goats	plants
darkness	wild asses	sea	sun (sunset)
dust	trees	mountains	breath
valleys	sunrise	rocks	
food	streams	creeping things	
night	cedars of Lebanon	earth	
death	work	coneys	
hills	birds of the air	living things	
wine	stork	grass	
all animals of the forest	evening	moon	
	branches	ships	
smoke	fir trees	cattle	
every wild animal	creatures	seasons	

10 In Real Life | Who Is God?

Read Romans 1:19-20a aloud. Say something like: *The Bible suggests that all these things can tell us something about God. What might the sun tell us about God? The birds? The trees? What might we learn about God from studying people (children, youth, elderly)? Creation depends on God to sustain it; what does this tell us about God?*

4. APPLY 10-15 minutes

>> **Option A and B:** (if you used *Option A* or *B* in Focus and Connect): Invite the group to go outside and find something *not* human made. Give the group a time limit (5-8 minutes), and a signal for when they should return to the room or to some appointed spot outside. When everyone is back, invite sharing what they found and what it might reveal about God.

Variation: (In case of bad weather): Do the above activity using photos, video, recorded music, or in imagination—imagine walking outside, looking around, finding something.

Ask: *What things in nature are hard to learn something about God from? Could even these things tell us something about God? What do thunderstorms, tornadoes, or earthquakes tell us about God?*

>> **Option C:** (if you used *Option C* in Focus and Connect): Pick questions from the Connect activity out of a basket and see if the list of created things from Psalm 104 can help answer any of those questions. (Some things in nature will give clues to the answers; some will give no clue.) One thing this tells us is that there is even more to God than what God created. Nature teaches about the Creator, but is not the Creator.

Variation: Invite your pastor or other church leader to spend some time with the group trying to discover what the Bible says about the questions raised on the cards.

5. RESPOND 5-10 minutes

>> **Option A:** (if you used *Option A*, Focus): Put all the drawings from the Focus activity into the center of the group. Ask people to bring into focus their special place in nature, then pray and meditate silently on what their special place might tell them about God. Offer (aloud) a prayer of praise for all these places in nature and what they tell people about God.

>> **Option B and C:** (if you used *Option B* or *C*, Focus): Invite the entire group to come back together and plan a service project to take care of God's creation—the earth or people.

>> **Option D (pair with any option chosen earlier in the session):**
As a group, give God names: Grower of trees, Builder of mountains, farmer, nursing mother. Address God this way for a least a week. What do we learn about God when we focus on God in a new way? If the group enjoys singing, close the session by singing some songs that celebrate nature and God as Creator.

"Ask the animals, and they will teach you; the birds, of the air, and they will tell you."

Job 12:7

"The entire material universe speaks of God's love, his boundless affection for us. Soil, water mountains: everything is, as it were, a caress of God."

Pope Francis
On Care for our Common Home, 84.

>>>
"Earth's crammed with heaven,
And every common bush afire with God;
But only he who sees takes off his shoes;
The rest sit round it and pluck blackberries."

Elizabeth Barrett Browning, *Aurora Leigh*

>>>
LOOK AHEAD

Session 2 offers the option of honoring future generations with a faith-forward project, such as planting a tree. Plan ahead.

INSIGHTS FROM SCRIPTURE

Romans declares that people cannot say they have seen and experienced the majesty of nature, and then claim they do not know God. God is invisible, yet God can clearly be *seen* and *understood* in creation.

Creation reveals how great, how awesome, and how loving God is. The psalmist expressed this with: "The heavens are telling the glory of God" (Psalm 19:1). But more than that, according to Psalm 104, God's continuing care for what was created reveals that God loves the created world, whether that is cats, snakes, trees, grandparents, or youth.

>> CREATION IS THE CLOTHING OF GOD

All people in all times and places have access to knowledge of God through the creation that surrounds them. They have no excuse for not knowing and honoring God. But some people today, as in Paul's day, have equated God with nature. The Bible does not offer us pantheism. God is not nature; God is *revealed* in nature.

As Bible commentator George A. F. Knight suggests, creation is the garment of God (*Psalms: Volume 2*). Like the purple or red robe of a monarch, creation reveals God's greatness to humanity. However, just as there is more to people than what they wear, so it is with God. Clothes tell a lot about a person, but are never identical to or a substitute for the total person.

>> LEVIATHAN

The presence of Leviathan (the sea monster) in the psalm presents the larger question of how monsters fit in creation. Some say Leviathan represents the chaos that was present before creation; others say Leviathan is a mythological monster. What about things in creation that are destructive, like hurricanes, tornadoes, floods, volcanoes, viruses and bacteria? What do monsters and tornadoes tell people about God?

These questions bring up fundamental questions that are difficult to answer: How can God be all-loving, all-good, and all-powerful, yet allow destruction in the world? "Part of its reverencing of the natural world," writes spirituality scholar J. Philip Newell in *The Book of Creation*, "is a respect also for creation's wildness and power....The naming of these as part of the mystery is neither to negate their fierceness nor to attempt to tame their wildness. It is to be aware of their power."

Another way to engage this tension is to observe how a "bad" event in one place and time may actually lead to good happening elsewhere. The disease of a grandmother causes a prodigal grandson to change his life; a massive flood inspires thousands of people to care for and serve each other. But such answers are not entirely satisfactory. People have free will, and sometimes bad things bring out the worst in people, not the best.

Perhaps tornadoes, earthquakes, and disease are divine reminders to people that they must lean on God, and demand that humans acknowledge who is truly Creator. Caught on a mountain hike during a massive thunderstorm, one youth group was not so much shocked that such things could happen, but reminded again that God is God, and humans are human. A further lesson about God is suggested in Psalm 104:26. The monster that is so fearsome (maybe even evil) in people's eyes, appears as a sporting, frolicking child to the all-powerful, all-knowing God. Could it be that God's perspective is so different, so much larger than ours? Could it be that God has a sense of humor and enjoys play? At the same time, it would be an error to think that God is capricious and somehow revels in human fear, pain, suffering or tragedy.

A classic treatment of these difficult questions that crop up again and again in life is this one by Rabbi Harold Kushner from his book, *When Bad Things Happen to Good People*: "Is there an answer to the question of why bad things happen to good people? That depends on what we mean by 'answer'. If we mean 'Is there an explanation which will make sense of it all?'… then there probably is no satisfying answer…. But the word 'answer' can also mean 'response' as well as 'explanation,' and in that sense, the response would be to forgive the world for not being perfect, to forgive God for not making a better world, to reach out to the people around us, and to go on living despite it all."

» EASY ACCESS

Nearly all youth have at one time or another been awestruck by the beauty of nature. Many enjoy sports, activities, and hobbies that involve the outdoors. Among those who report that they have experienced God's presence, many say the experience occurred in nature. Beginning this unit with a session that invites participants to learn about God through creation provides an accessible place for them to open up to how and where they experience God.

The World According to Psalm 104

Listen as Psalm 104:10-32 is read, then write in the space below ALL the things created by God that were named.

>>> **SESSION 2**

GOD KEEPS PROMISES >>>

>> KEY VERSES

"I also established my covenant with them, to give them the land of Canaan, the land in which they resided as aliens. 'I will bring you into the land that I swore to give to Abraham, Isaac, and Jacob; I will give it to you for a possession. I am the Lord.'" (Exodus 6:4, 8)

>> FAITH STORY

Exodus 6:1-8

>> FAITH FOCUS

When Moses and Aaron first demanded that Pharaoh free the Israelite slaves, Pharaoh only tightened his grip. So Moses complained to God that the divine plan for freedom had gone awry. God assured Moses that divine authority still honored the promises made to previous generations. God liberated the Israelites and gave them a way out of bondage, revealing that God keeps promises even after hundreds of years—even when God's children betray the covenant, God is faithful.

>> SESSION GOAL

In a culture where people demand immediate gratification and often fail to keep promises, challenge participants to understand God as trustworthy and responsive.

>> Materials needed and advance preparation

- Stack of magazines and box of paperclips (*Option A*, Focus)

- Copies of both handout sheets and pencils/markers (*Option B*, Focus and *Option A*, Apply)

- Cards prepared with Interviewer questions (*Option A*, Connect)

- Bibles

- Signs with dates on them (see Explore the Bible)

- Index cards and pencils (*Option A*, Apply)

- Chalkboard/chalk or newsprint/marker

- Obtain a sapling and plan with the appropriate people in the parish about where to plant it (*Option A*, Respond).

TEACHING PLAN

1. FOCUS 6-10 minutes

>> **Option A:** Pair up or form small groups. Then direct people to the stack of magazines to look for **ads that make promises**, and paperclip the pages, so they can find the ads easily when they share them. As participants share with the group the ads they've found, have them tell:

- what the ad promises;
- whether or not they believe the product/service can really fulfill the promise.

"People say the worst thing about broken promises is...

- the hurt that is left behind
- the feeling of betrayal
- finding out that someone is undependable."

"People who keep promises best are...

- my best friend.
- me.
- family."

Option B: Distribute copies of the first handout sheet and pencils. Invite participants to write down two promises that people make to each other that they do not always keep. (Examples include: to pick someone up at a certain time, to clean a room, to take someone shopping, to pay a bill, to be in touch later that day, to love and be faithful until death.) Then have the group arrange their promises in order from least important to most important by standing up and arranging themselves in a line or by placing the papers in order on the floor or on a wall.

2. CONNECT 10-15 minutes

Option A: Invite the group to explore more deeply the nature of promises. Pair up, with one person taking the role of the **Average Youth**. The other is the **Interviewer**. Give each **Interviewer** a pencil and set of cards prepared ahead with the questions below.

Instruct the **Interviewer** to ask the questions, and record answers right on the card. Assure the **Average Youth** the answers will be shared with the whole group, but anonymously.

- When is it tempting to put off keeping a promise?
- When is it tempting to break a promise?
- How do you know for sure when someone has broken a promise?
- What is the worst thing about a broken promise?
- How much time must elapse between making a promise and keeping a promise before the promise is declared broken?
- If a parent promises to give a fifth grade child a trip to the Grand Canyon, but does not take them until they are 45 and have children of their own, does that constitute a broken promise? Why or why not?

Allow about 5 minutes for the interviews. Then collect the cards from the **Interviewers**, mix them up, and pass them out again. Have participants share responses to the questions from the interview response cards, or from their own ideas.

Option B: Invite people to think more about promises. Take a survey using the following scenarios.

Designate one end of the room as "strongly agree" and the other end as "strongly disagree." Invite people to position themselves at either end of the room or somewhere in between based on their responses to the scenarios. Prompt discussion after each scenario by requesting explanations for why people chose their spot. Augment with questions from **Option A**.

1. One morning before school, Charity promises her mother she will mow the lawn. That day passes, and another. That evening the lawn is still not mowed. This is a broken promise.
2. A parent promised to give their fifth grade son a trip to the Grand Canyon. The son is now 45 and has children of his own, and the parent makes plans for the Grand Canyon trip. But the promise is already broken.
3. Blake tells Derek he is thinking of hurting himself and makes Derek promise not to tell his parents. Derek is really concerned about Blake, so he calls Blake's grandparents and tells them. This is a broken promise.

3. EXPLORE THE BIBLE 12-18 minutes

Shift to this activity by saying: *It's very disappointing when promises remain unfulfilled or are broken. But we know from the Bible that God always keeps promises; it just may take quite a while.... The question is the timing.*

Prepare participants to hear part of a speech given by God from the book of Exodus by challenging the group to listen for the following information:

- Who made the promise? (God)
- To whom was the promise made? (Abraham; or Abraham, Isaac, and Jacob)
- What was promised? (the land of Canaan)

Then read Exodus 6:2-4 aloud. Have participants answer the three questions above. Then fill in the rest of the story, summarizing:

God had promised Abraham that his descendants would possess the land of Canaan (Genesis 15:18). But Abraham's sons died. His later descendants became slaves in Egypt under Pharaoh. Hundreds of years had passed and they still struggled in oppression. Moses was called by God to help the Israelites escape slavery. Moses made some attempts that made things worse for everybody. The people got angry with Moses, and Moses began to doubt his mission. In this speech, God was telling Moses that the people of Israel would be freed. God reassured Moses that the promises made to Abraham long ago were remembered, and that Moses was to continue to help the promise be fulfilled.

Acknowledge that God took quite a while to fulfill the part of the covenant about the land. God's promise to Abraham was not even fulfilled within the lifetime of his grandchildren or great-grandchildren.

Experience this as a human timeline. Mark one end of the room or have one participant stand with a sign that says "2200 B.C.E." Invite the rest of the group to walk with you, with **one step representing about 50 years** (2 steps = 100 years, and so on), from promise made to promise fulfilled. A timeline follows below:

2 steps	2091 B.C.E.	God promises Abraham
1 step	2066 B.C.E.	Abraham's son, Isaac born
1 step	2006 B.C.E.	Abraham's grandsons Jacob and Esau born
¼ step	991 B.C.E.	15 or so years later, Abraham dies
2 steps	1915 B.C.E.	Abraham's great-grandson Joseph born
1 step	1886 B.C.E.	Isaac dies
½ step	1859 B.C.E.	Jacob dies
1 step	1805 B.C.E.	Joseph dies
6 steps	1526 B.C.E.	Moses born
2 steps	1446 B.C.E.	Moses leads the exodus
1 step	1406 B.C.E.	Moses dies; Israelites enter Canaan

Help participants understand that the promise made to Abraham was a *covenant*, or a two-way agreement between unequals, imposed by God, whose responsibility was to be God to give Abraham's descendants a home land.

Abraham's responsibility, and that of his descendants, was to *walk with God*, believing and obeying (Genesis 17:1), and to circumcise all males (Genesis 17:11-12) as a sign of this covenant.

Although the Israelites were not always faithful and obedient to their part of the covenant, all in all it took over 600 years between promise and fulfillment. Generations and generations of people were born and died before a home was gained. Discuss:

- *Does a promise fulfilled after 600 years count? Why or why not?*
- *How does it make you feel knowing that God remembers a promise even after 600 years?*
- *How would you feel if God made a promise to you and your descendants that would not be fulfilled until the year 2600 C.E. or so?*

Before moving on to Apply, make the following points clearly. Most of Western culture is impatient and demands immediate gratification. If a promise is made and then not delivered quick, like fast-food or by next-day air, we complain. The Bible, however, reveals that God's promises were made to the community, not just to the individual, and that fulfillment even after 600 years counts!

"Community" included not only a group of people in one generation, but also the lives in generations to come. Participating in God's promise today means participants will work for the good of a people, an earth, a time, and a world they might never live to see.

> **"Community" includes not just one generation, but also the lives in generations to come. Participating in God's promise today means working for the good of a people, an earth, a time, and a world we might never live to see.**

4. APPLY 10-15 minutes

Point out that God has made promises in the Bible that they may or may not see fulfilled in their lifetimes. Examples:

- the coming of a new heaven and a new earth (Isaiah 65:17; Revelation 21:1)
- nation will not take up sword against nation and they will not train for war anymore (Micah 4:3)
- fear will be banished (Micah 4:4)
- the Lord will come again (Matthew 24:42)
- those who mourn will be comforted (Matthew 5:4)
- the pure in heart will see God (Matthew 5:8)
- all things work together for good for those who love God (Romans 8:28)

Remind participants that, like Moses, people of faith are called to participate in fulfilling God's promises, even though this generation may never live to see it happen.

>> **Option A:** Distribute pencils and copies of the second handout sheet. Have people follow the instructions there. Invite participants individually to finish the statements with as many things as they can think of: "I would like to promise future generations that..." Give one or two examples if participants seem stuck, such as "the world will live in peace," "health care will be available to all," "no more need for drugs and violence," "climate change will be no threat," "family life will improve," etc. Allow 5 minutes for thinking and writing. Then ask participants to star each one that they think aligns with God's intention.

Highlight the reminder on the handout sheet that our covenant with God is similar to that of Abraham's descendants—we will walk in the path of the Creator, believe, and act with obedience. In other words, we are called, like Moses, to help God's promises come into being. Go to **Option A**, Respond.

>> **Option B:** Think further about the idea of a two-way promise or covenant. Divide the group into four small groups and make newsprint and markers available. (If you have fewer groups, double up on the relationship categories that follow.) Instruct each group to write or draw the responsibilities of each of the parties in one of the following two-way agreements (assign one relationship to each group):

- parent and youth
- teacher and student
- coach and athlete
- God and faithful disciple

Allow 5-7 minutes to work, then have each group share their descriptions. Go to **Option B**, Respond.

5. RESPOND 8-15 minutes

>> **Option A:** Brainstorm together about what youth can do individually or together to help God's promises come into being for a future generation. Write all ideas on newsprint or a chalkboard. Then pick one idea and plan together something the group could do for a future generation that would help bring about God's purposes (like plant a tree, start a recycling program at your church, become trained in mediation and conflict resolution, make a "Good News" time capsule). What first steps can the group take *in this moment* to launch the idea?

>> **Option B:** Invite people to get comfortable and close their eyes as you lead them in a guided meditation to help them focus on *covenant*. Write a new one or adapt the one that follows. Pause for 6-8 seconds at the end of each phrase.

> *Begin with noticing breath—the* ruach—*Hebrew for breath—of the Source of Life and Being...*
>
> *When thoughts arise, as thoughts do, planning, remembering, simple let them pass*
>
> *Just this breath, just this now, just this. Awake and alert.*
>
> *Now switch focus to the word covenant. What do you notice about what this word does in you? What is your felt response when you hear this word?*
>
> *What if you put this word in your mouth?*
>
> *What might it taste like?*
>
> *What is its texture like? Roll it around.*
>
> *If you notice thoughts arising, bring focus back to this word.*
>
> *What happens if you swallow this word? How does it go down?*
>
> *What is covenant like as it settles in your belly?*
>
> *As it gets digested, moves into your bloodstream and courses through your body?*
>
> *How does it change your energy level?*
>
> *How does it affect your experience of the Creator?*
>
> *How does it affect your experience of your neighbor, now that this word is such an integral part of you?*
>
> *Now return to noticing your breathing...*
>
> *How does the word covenant affect your respiration? Does it speed it up or slow it down?*
>
> *Follow your breath. Just this. This prayer. This word, covenant. It reminds you that you are loved. It reminds you that you are connected to the Creator and the path of Life....*
>
> *And the people opened their eyes and said AMEN.*

LOOK AHEAD

For the next session, contact someone to talk to the group about how they experience God's presence (*Option B*, Respond).

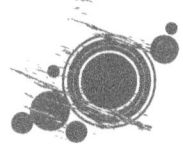

In Real Life | Who Is God?

INSIGHTS FROM SCRIPTURE

Moses was called by God to help lead the enslaved Israelites out of Egypt. After his initial failure with Pharaoh, the captives complained that Moses had made things worse, because now they had to make bricks without straw. Moses was caught between God's call to lead the Israelites and the people wanting Moses to just stay out of it. Moses was between a Rock and a hard place, and he was not happy about it.

God listened to Moses complain that the divine plan for freedom had gone awry. Then in Exodus 6, God spoke directly to Moses, assuring him that divine authority still honored the promises made to previous generations. God liberated the Israelites and gave them a way out of bondage, revealing that God keeps promises even after hundreds of years—even when God's children betray the covenant, God is faithful.

》 COVENANT

The biblical concept of covenant dominates this passage—an agreement between unequals imposed by God, whose responsibility was to be God's (Genesis 17:8) to give them a homeland.

Abraham's responsibility, and that of his descendants, was to *walk with God*, believing and obeying (Genesis 17:1) and to circumcise all males (Genesis 17:11-12) as an outward sign of this covenant.

》 WHEN FULFILLMENT IS DELAYED

God remembers promises made to previous generations and is faithful in fulfilling them. God does not forget these promises. To a generation of youth who have seen a lot of commitments and promises broken (marriage and political vows, for example), experiencing God as faithful, One who keeps promises, may provide security and stability.

But young people, like much of North American culture, are impatient and demand immediate gratification. How will youth respond to God when it appears promises are not fulfilled within their lifetimes? The promise made to Abraham in Genesis 12:7 was "to your descendants." Abraham responded with joy and worship. One possible response to unfulfilled promises is trust, patience, obedience, hope, joy, and worship. Another possibility is frustration, impatience, giving up, seeking immediate pleasure from the material world. Which will youth choose?

》 NO BURNING BUSH

Abraham was happy for the bright future of his descendants. What do youth hope for those who come after them? Another challenge to youth comes from Moses, who was called to help make God's promises a reality for future generations. No amazing burning bush appeared again during those long years of the exodus. There was no recorded epiphany, but Moses heard God's voice and responded.

Can youth live so unselfishly? Are they willing to work for the good of an earth and a time and people they'll never meet? God calls us, like Moses, to help fulfill divine promises. What are we willing and able to do to help God's promises become reality?

Broken Promises

Exploring tough questions facing youth today

Write down two promises that people make to each other that they do not always keep. (Examples include: to pick someone up at a certain time, to clean a room, to take someone shopping, to pay a bill, to be in touch later in the day, to love and be faithful until death.)

>>>

"If the only prayer you would say in your whole life is 'thank you,' that would suffice."

Meister Eckhart, 13th-century Christian mystic

HOW TO EXPERIENCE GOD'S FAITHFULNESS? PRACTICE GRATITUDE...

End your day with this practice. Name at least one thing you are grateful for, small or large, and thank God. Another way is to pause periodically in your day and notice something good within your sight or hearing, and say yes to it. "Yes to that spreading tree, Yes to that flying ball, Yes to the warm blanket, Yes to the raspberry." As you do this, notice what happens inside you.

Permission is granted to photocopy this handout for use with this session.

Future Promises

Exploring tough questions facing youth today

Our covenant with God is similar to that of Abraham's descendants— we will walk in the path of the Creator, believe, and act with obedience. In other words, we are called, like Moses, to help God's promises come into being.

Finish the statement with as many things as you can think of: "I would like to promise future generations that..."

Examples:
  Health care will be available to all.
  Climate change will be no threat.

Next, star each one you think aligns with God's intention.

Who Is God? : Session 2

 **OK to photocopy**

Permission is granted to photocopy this handout for use with this session.

>>> **SESSION 3**

GOD IS PRESENT

>> KEY VERSES

Where can I go from your spirit? Or where can I flee from your presence? If I ascend to heaven, you are there; if I make my bed in Sheol, you are there. If I take the wings of the morning and settle at the farthest limits of the sea, even there your hand shall lead me, and your right hand shall hold me fast. (Psalm 139:7-10)

>> FAITH STORY

Psalm 139:1-18

>> FAITH FOCUS

The psalmist understood that God creates humans in a wonderful, mysterious way, knows them intimately, and is present in all places and circumstances. This knowledge came from the psalmist's personal experience of God in the ups and downs of everyday life. Immersed in an intimate relationship with the divine Presence, the psalmist describes a model for participants who desire a close relationship with God.

>> SESSION GOAL

In a time when people (even parents) often are too busy to "be present," help participants to understand that the ultimate relationship of life is with God, who is closer than we are to ourselves, whether or not that Presence is felt or recognized.

TEACHING PLAN

1. FOCUS 12-15 minutes

Pair up, and have each duo choose a "speaker." Tell the speakers they will have 3 minutes to tell the other person something. Participants who normally have no problem talking to one another might be speechless. Give them some possible topics such as:

- What I did yesterday
- My favorite or least favorite teacher
- The best vacation I ever had
- My opinion of church
- Something I'm looking forward to

>> Materials needed and advance preparation

- Writing paper and pencils
- Copies of the handout sheet for Session 3
- Bibles (consider using a paraphrase)
- Prepare "Thought/Feeling" cards and "Psalm" cards (or mark Bibles—see Explore the Bible)
- Chalkboard/chalk or newsprint/markers
- Reserve the sanctuary or chapel for 10 minutes (one choice in *Option A, Respond*).
- Invite a guest to talk about how they experience God's presence (*Option B, Respond*).
- Choose ahead of time a way of sharing God's presence with others, and make plans to carry it out after the session (*Option C, Respond*).

"If God is always with me and knows everything about me...

- I feel understood."
- I feel safe and protected."
- I'm freaked out if God is watching everything I do."
- It makes me nervous, because I don't always want God with me. (But who is God going to tell?)"

At the end of 3 minutes, call time, and give those who listened paper to write down everything they heard the other say. Give them a few minutes (or until they are ready to stop trying to remember). Then have the speaker "correct" the listener's paper. (*Alternative:* Have listeners respond orally to the group about what they heard rather than writing it.)

Option for small groups: Do not break up into pairs. Have the whole group discuss a topic. At the end of 5 minutes, give each person pencil and paper. Tell them to write down (or reconstruct orally) as much as they remember of what each person said.

Ask: *How many listeners got pretty much everything right? What did you miss? Why didn't you remember everything? What made it hard/easy? How many speakers think they had a good listener?*

2. CONNECT 10 minutes

Distribute copies of the handout sheet and pencils. Tell the participants to circle the five best listeners on the list they find there. Then rank the circled ones from one to five (one being the best listener). When finished, invite sharing about the top listeners and why. Explore any alternate opinions.

Then ask: *How can you tell if someone is really listening to you? What are the signs? How do you know when someone is not listening?*

3. EXPLORE THE BIBLE 10 minutes

Shift to this activity by saying: *Part of being a good listener is the skill of being present. It is a rare and wonderful thing to find someone who will always be present to listen. The psalmist found this in a relationship with God.*

Have people listen carefully for what the psalmist is trying to express about God, as you read Psalm 139:1-10. (Consider using a paraphrase or translation participants may not be immediately familiar with, such as Nan Merrill's *Psalms for Praying: An Invitation to Wholeness.*) Invite responses. Reinforce that the psalmist was convinced of God's presence in good times and bad, despite obedience or disobedience.

Ask: *How does this make you feel, knowing that you cannot escape from God anywhere?* Depending on the maturity and comfort level of your group, you may want to treat this as a rhetorical question. *How did the psalmist respond to this state of affairs?* This writer found hope, even wonder and joy, in the fact that God knew everything and was always present.

Say something like: *Certain of God's presence, the psalmist talked to God in all kinds of situations.* Invite the group to discover some of the thoughts and feelings the writers of the psalms shared with God. Use your prepared **Thought/Feeling cards** by writing each of the words below on a separate index card. Also prepare **Psalm cards** by copying each of the sets of verses below on a separate index card, or mark Bibles ahead of time. (Again, consider using a paraphrase or different Bible translation to prepare the cards.) If your group has more than 12 members, add more or make duplicate copies of the ones below.

If you have a group of more than six, give half the participants **Thought/Feeling cards** and the other half **Psalm cards** or marked Bibles. (If you have fewer than 12, some people will have two cards.) Have people note whether they hold Thought/Feeling cards or Psalm cards that express feelings. Now, everyone moves around the room and find the person who has a card that matches theirs.

If you have a group of less than six, people can work together to match the Thought/Feeling cards to Psalm cards.

Thought/Feeling cards	Psalm cards or marked Bibles
Thankful for advice	Psalm 16:7-8
Ridiculed, disliked	Psalm 22:6-7
Parents don't care or understand	Psalm 27:9-10
In trouble, but not afraid	Psalm 46:1-3
Guilty, sorry for sin	Psalm 51:1-2
Wanting an enemy destroyed	Psalm 55:15

Allow 3-5 minutes to match the cards, then have pairs read aloud the psalm verses and the feeling that goes with it. Remind the group that the psalmist talked about *all* these things to God.

4. APPLY 10-15 minutes

>> **Option A:** Invite participants to pick a **Thought/Feeling** or **Psalm card** that appeals to them. Turn back to the handout sheet, and give them a little time to write or doodle a situation in which they might want to say things similar to what the psalmist said to God. Invite sharing of the work as they are willing.

Some possible follow-up questions (or make up your own):

- At what times might you not want to talk to God?
- Should people share everything with God? Why or why not?
- What kinds of things would it be difficult to share with God?
- Would it be easier to share things with God or a parent?

>> **Option B:** Have participants form groups of three or four. Have each group pick a **Thought/Feeling card** and **Psalm card** pair. Give them time to prepare and present a role play of a situation that might cause them to want to say similar things to God as the psalmists did.

>> **Option C:** Hold a debate concerning **one** of the following statements:

- Believers should tell God absolutely everything.
- It is easier to share things with God than with a parent.

Divide the group into two. Assign one group to prepare arguments in support of the statement, and the other to prepare reasons why the statement is wrong. Give groups 5 minutes to prepare. Line up chairs opposite each other, and give sides 5-10 minutes to debate.

In order for the debate to run more smoothly, allow one side to make opening arguments without interruption. Then allow the other group to respond for the same time period without interruption. For the remaining time, allow open discussion.

5. RESPOND 10-20 minutes

Say something like: *It's usually pretty easy to tell whether or not other people are listening to us. Maybe not so easy with God. Does God really hear us? Is God really interested? David was one person who wrote poetry—called psalms—about what it was like to talk with and feel God present and listening to him.*

As a group, brainstorm about what would convince them that God is present and listening, writing all ideas on the chalkboard or on newsprint. If necessary, offer examples: hearing

"**Learn to stay before [God] in silence, to read and meditate on the Bible, especially the Gospels, to converse with Him everyday in order to feel His presence of friendship and love.**"

Pope Francis,

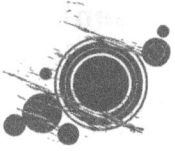

God's voice, experiencing a miracle, feeling God through your conscience, worshipping with others, being able to do something that you know you could not do without God's help (save a life, forgive someone, confront someone, serve others, witness). Ask: *How do we know God is present (in our lives, in the world)? How do you think David knew?*

Now choose one of the following options:

>> **Option A:** Try to help participants experience God's presence. This could be risky and make both you and your participants feel vulnerable. Nothing may happen for participants, but something may. Try to be relaxed and encouraging about it. Three possibilities are listed below:

- *Journal writing:* Give each person lined paper and a pencil. Find a quiet spot to write a journal entry about something that happened in the past week. Give a few minutes to write, then put down pencils, close the eyes, and listen for what God might be saying.
- *Meditation on nature:* Take participants outside, and assign them to find something in nature to focus on (a leaf, a blade of grass, a tree, an insect). Give them a few moments to find something. Then invite them to be seated and focus for five minutes on the thing they have chosen. Do not give any more instruction than that. Tell them to simply wait and observe what happens.
- *Prayer in a sanctuary or chapel:* Take participants to a chapel or sanctuary, lead them in a prayer like the one below while they sit silently and wait.

God, we have a lot of things to tell you. Hear us now as we talk to you. (Pause.) *We want to feel your presence, loving God. We want to know you are with us and have heard each one of us. We want to be aware of what you want us to know. Help us be patient and quiet, willing to wait on you.* (Pause for several minutes.) *Amen.*

>> **Option B:** If the group is not yet ready to try something like **Option A**, invite someone from your parish to come in and talk to the group about how they experience God's presence.

>> **Option C:** Brainstorm ways in which believers *do* or *can* share God's presence with others who may have difficulty experiencing it. What might it look like to express this tangibly? With others?

"God, who is everywhere, never leaves us. Yet He seems sometimes to be present, sometimes to be absent. If we do not know Him well, we do not realize that He may be more present to us when He is absent than when He is present."

Thomas Merton
No Man Is an Island

INSIGHTS FROM SCRIPTURE

Many psalms are congregational hymns and poems, and others, like Psalm 139, are deeply personal expressions, almost like a journal or diary entry. This writer is no theologian professing a doctrine—this is simple awe and wonder at being in God's presence—everywhere. The psalmist is interested in how these things converge in the intimacy of a personal relationship with the Divine.

>> GOD KNOWS EVERYTHING!

God has searched each person. Does God have X-ray vision? Has God "scanned" everyone's soul? The psalmist did not know—and neither does anyone know now—how God does it, but God knows everyone's desires, fears, and failures, because God is the heart of Life in each being. The experience of an all-knowing God did not bring out fear in the psalmist, but instead filled him with wonder, joy, and love toward God. Yet relating to a God that knows everything can sometimes be uncomfortable—we may want to hide, naked and guilty, as Adam and Eve attempted in the garden of Eden.

>> GOD IS PRESENT EVERYWHERE

Another mixed blessing confronts youth in that God is always present with them; there is nowhere they can get away from God. There is likely part of each of us that may not even want God to be present all the time. But the psalmist found this far more comforting than threatening, because God's presence meant God's constant love. So radical is God's love, the psalmist said, that even in Sheol (the place of the dead), God would be present and loving.

>> DON'T FENCE ME IN!

Youth have a lot of freedom (and they enjoy it)! How will they respond to a God who knows everything about them, a God from whom they cannot hide or get away? If they feel misunderstood and alone, it could be a comforting thought. If they have lies and secrets to hide, they may feel fenced in and want to run away.

The best-case scenario is that participants will clearly hear the message that God has claimed them from the time they were formed in their mother's womb because God loves them. Can we help youth discover that being fenced in—"hemmed in" as in Psalm 139—by God's loving presence is quite another thing from being trapped?

Youth are precious to God. Even if they are trapped in the darkness of drugs, drinking, materialism, or sexual promiscuity, God is present with them. If they are in the depths of depression or despair, in trouble, rejected by friends, horrified at what is in their own hearts, God loves them and wants to relate to them. The writers of the psalms talked to God in all kinds of moods and situations. Today's youth can do the same, and they can trust that God will be present with them, wherever they are.

Lend Me Your Ear!

Exploring tough questions facing youth today

Consider the list of people below. Circle the 5 people whom you've experienced to be the best listeners. Then rank the five circled listeners from 1-5, with 1 being the best listener.

____ Boys
____ Girls
____ Mother
____ Father
____ Teacher
____ School counselor
____ Friend
____ Brother
____ Sister
____ Grandmother
____ Grandfather
____ Pastor
____ Youth group leader
____ Coach
____ Music instructor
____ Me
____ Cousin

A few listening guidelines

- Let the person know you are paying attention through eye contact, body language, and occasional brief comments.
- Avoid thinking about your response while the person is talking.
- If someone is sharing something intense and personal, don't share an "I can top that" story.
- Don't interrupt.
- Avoid giving advice until they ask for it—just listen.
- Sometimes the person may say something important to them even if it doesn't seem important to you.

Here's what I want to say...

Pick a **Thought/Feeling** or **Psalm card** that appeals to you. On the back, write or doodle a situation in which you might want to say things similar to what the psalmist said to God. Share your work if you're willing.

Who Is God? : Session 3

Permission is granted to photocopy this handout for use with this session.

>>> **SESSION 4**

GOD IS LIKE... >>>

>> KEY VERSE
The Lord is my *shepherd*. (Psalm 23:1a)

>> FAITH STORY
Psalm 23
Various scriptures that name similes or metaphors for God

>> FAITH FOCUS
The psalmist compared God to a shepherd, which emphasized God's care for people in both joy and tragedy. The psalmist also said God was like a gracious host who exhibited lavish hospitality in the face of enemies. The psalmist used metaphor and simile to describe God. There are both strengths and limits to describing God through figures of speech.

>> SESSION GOAL
Help participants to understand how metaphors function in understanding God, and to consider both the strengths and weaknesses of using these comparisons to describe the divine Mystery.

TEACHING PLAN

>> Materials needed and advance preparation

- Cup or soda pop can (one choice in *Option A*, Focus)
- Bibles
- Copies of the handout sheet for Session 4
- Prepare slips of paper with scripture references and bring a hat or a basket from which participants can draw them (see Explore).
- Chalkboard/chalk or newsprint/markers
- Objects to help participants depict contemporary ways of experiencing God (*Option A*, Apply)
- Writing paper, mural paper, and markers/pencils (*Options* in Apply)
- Song Books (*Option C*, Respond)

1. FOCUS 5-15 minutes

>> **Option A:** Give participants tasks that are impossible to perform, but do not tell them they are impossible. Examples follow, but your group might think up new ones. Try each one for just a few minutes, except where there is a specific time limit.

- *Stuck to the Wall:* Stand up straight with right foot and right shoulder against the wall. Tell them to try to move the left leg without falling, taking a step, or allowing their arm to leave the wall. Then tell them to stand with the left foot and right shoulder against the wall. Tell them to try to lift the right leg.

- *The Unreachable Cup:* Challenge participants to stand up straight with their backs and heels against the wall. (This may also be done with pairs of participants standing back to back.) Place a cup or a pop can about 10-20 inches on the floor in front of each participant's feet. Participants will try to bend over and pick up the cup or can without falling. They must keep their heels against the wall (or against their partner's heels), and they may not bend their knees or have any part of their feet leave the floor.

>>>

"I think that people need to come up with their own image of God, whatever they feel comfortable with. For me, it is not always the same. I feel more comfort when I think of God as a large woman in a rocking chair on whose lap I can sit. She can rock me back and forth, hum a peaceful tune, and caress my hair as she listens to me. God is also a fresh breeze, a springtime flower, the touch of a friend. I think it is very healthy to open up our minds to new images. Of God. Of the world. Of each other. God is a mystery. Isn't that exciting?! Another one I like: God is like a warm bed."

Tina Rieman, student

- *Tongue Twisters:* Say one of the following six times quickly in a row. **Note:** Insist that they be said quickly, or they won't be impossible to do.

  Six gray geese on green grass grazing.
  Six thick thistle sticks.
  Round and round the rugged rock the ragged rascal ran.
  Copper coffee pot.
  Ziggy Jazinski.

  (From *Fun with Skits, Stunts, and Stories,* by Helen and Larry Eisenberg)

- *Speed Talking:* Tell participants to get in pairs. Challenge one participant to tell their partner every single thing they did last month. Tell them they have 2 minutes, and time them.

Go to **Option A**, Connect.

>> **Option B:** Read the story below, or have someone in the group read it.

The Blind Men and the Elephant

Six blind men were brought to "see" an elephant. "It is very much like a wall," said the first man as he touched the side of the elephant. "It is very like a spear," said the second man as he stroked the elephant's tusk. The third man took the elephant's squirming trunk in his hand and said, "It is very much like a snake!" "Nonsense!" the fourth man shouted. Stretching his arms about one of the legs, he concluded, "This wondrous beast is very much like a tree!" The fifth man, touching the elephant's ear, cried out, "Even the blindest can tell this animal is very much like a fan." Grabbing the tail, the sixth man assured his friends that "the elephant is really very like a rope!"

Go to **Option B**, Connect.

2. CONNECT 5 minutes

>> **Option A:** Say: *Do you think the task (or tasks) was impossible? Name some things that are impossible to do.* (Examples: for human beings to fly like birds, or walk on water, or live without oxygen). *How do you know when something is impossible?*

>> **Option B:** Discuss what made it difficult for the blind men to discover what they were experiencing.

3. EXPLORE THE BIBLE 15 minutes

Shift to this activity by saying: *What makes it impossible for us to describe or define God in words or a picture? Where can we get clues to be able to communicate about a Mystery?*

Remind participants what simile and metaphor are. Both are figures of speech based on comparison. Simile uses *like* or *as*. Example: Love is like a red rose. Metaphor transfers qualities of one term to something it does not literally apply to. Example: The game of life.

Now invite participants to find clues to God's identity by using similes and metaphors from the Bible. Distribute handout sheets, and use the first line, Psalm 23, to demonstrate the process. Read (or have someone read) Psalm 23. Name the metaphors (images) for God in this passage. Think together about what these images tell us. Mirror the handout sheet chart on chalkboard or newsprint (to be completed as a group later) with the headings **Bible Passage, Simile/Metaphor,** and **Reveals What About God?**

Put slips of paper, prepared with Bible passages **only** (not the image), in a hat or basket, and have people draw one out, and work alone, in pairs, or in small groups to complete their portion of the chart. Then report to the whole, filling in the rest of the chart on both the handouts and the board or newsprint.

Bible Passage	Simile/Metaphor	Reveals What About God?
Example: Psalm 23	Shepherd, gracious host	Comforts; provides; generous
Luke 15:8-10	Woman searching for lost coin	Seeks the lost; celebrates the found
Luke 15:11-24	Forgiving father of lost child	Loves the lost; forgives
Psalm 31:3	Rock and fortress	Solid; strong; foundation
Psalm 3:3	Shield	Protector; strong
Matthew 20:1-16	Owner of a vineyard	Generous; great mercy seems unfair
Luke 14:15-24	Man having a great banquet	Invites all to the divine Presence
John 15:1-2	Father, gardener	Lovingly tends; judges and prunes
Psalm 27:1	Light, salvation, stronghold	Guides in darkness; saves
Psalm 90:1	Dwelling place	Provides; place to be safe and secure
Deut. 32:11-12	Eagle caring for its young	Nurtures like a parent
Revelation 21:6	Alpha and Omega	Beginning and end; all-encompassing

Discuss as a whole group: *What makes these images helpful in discovering who God is? Are there characteristics that are true of these images that would **not** be true of God? What are they? What are the dangers of using images like this to describe God? Is it possible to find a name, image, or description of God that is not a metaphor? Why or why not? Is "father" a metaphor for God? Why or why not? In what ways do we limit God?*

4. APPLY 10-15 minutes

>> **Option A:** Give participants some items (flashlight, key, play dough, chair, crown, tape, matches, soap, water, and others you think of). Tell participants to create their own contemporary metaphors for God, building or sculpting something using the items you brought, or think of their own. They could also write a line or two of poetry about God, using the items to stimulate their thinking. Ask them to evaluate the strengths and weaknesses of their metaphors/similes (such as what parts of this metaphor fit God? What qualities of the comparison do not fit?).

>> **Option B:** Provide large sheets of mural paper and markers. Invite groups of participants to create drawings of God based on biblical metaphors or their own contemporary figures of speech.

"Almost everything said of God is unworthy, for the very reason that it is capable of being said."

Pope Gregory the Great, *Magna moralia*

"We do not have a little tame domestic God, thank God, but we do have a huge, wild, dangerous God—dangerous of course only if we think that God ought to be manageable and safe; a God of almost manic creativity, ingenuity and enthusiasm; a Big-Enough God, who is also a supremely generous and patient God; a God of beauty and chance and solidarity."

Sara Maitland,
A Big-Enough God.

5. RESPOND 10 minutes

>> **Option A:** Using the contemporary "sculpted" metaphors, poems, doodles, or mural drawings, allow people a few minutes to trade until they get someone else's they can connect with. Then invite participants to focus in silence on that image of God, and what it might mean for them in the coming week. Allow 3-5 minutes of focused silence, and close with a brief spoken prayer.

>> **Option B:** Work together as a group to write a psalm on one of the contemporary metaphors participants create. Psalm 23 or Psalm 46 could be models. Pray the psalm to close the session.

>> **Option C:** If the group likes to sing, search song books for images from lyrics that speak to them. This could be informal, with participants naming metaphors aloud each time they find one. Pick one song to sing as a closing.

INSIGHTS FROM SCRIPTURE

It is impossible for human beings to describe or define God completely. But God can be known and understood to some degree. How do people begin to understand what God is like? One way is to start with who people are and things people see, experience, and understand, and then make verbal comparisons (simile and metaphor). Another method involves ascribing human characteristics to God (anthropomorphism).

>> THE POWER OF FIGURES OF SPEECH

That's exactly the technique David used in Psalm 23, when he compared God to two common human images: a good shepherd and a gracious host. The image of shepherd would have had special meaning to David, who had spent time in the fields watching sheep. Like a shepherd, God cares for us, protects us, guides us, and comforts us. The gracious host metaphor teaches that God is generous (cup overflows) and hospitable. God wishes good things for human beings, gives them plenty (bountiful table), and provides shelter (the house of the Lord). The comparisons used in figures of speech can give a concrete, down-to-earth handle on God's identity. Many of them present visual pictures as well. These kinds of images give us practical, concrete ways to understand God.

>> THE LIMITS OF METAPHOR

But comparisons are limited, and this is especially important to remember when using metaphors for God. Take the shepherd example. What are the limits of this comparison? Does God really have a beard, wear robes, and carry a staff? Does God really see people as no better than a bunch of stupid sheep? The answer to both questions is probably no. Metaphors are always limited. When working with such comparisons, it is helpful also to think of contrasts. What about God is not like a human shepherd or a host?

OUTDATED METAPHORS?

The language of a shepherd would have spoken clearly to the people of the psalmist's day. Flocks of sheep grazing on a hillside with a shepherd watching over them would have been a common scene. But urbanized people today may not connect readily with the shepherd imagery. Are there contemporary metaphors that would give clearer ideas? Although the father metaphor for God gives a strong visual, a recognizable image, what are its limits, especially for those who have experienced a father's absence or even abuse? How can we use metaphor to highlight how male and female are both created in God's image?

Hymns offer powerful metaphors. Hundreds of years ago (1633) poet George Herbert wrote an entire hymn (about Jesus), using nine metaphors and only single-syllable words, except for one:

> Come, my Way, my Truth, my Life:
> Such a way as gives us breath;
> Such a truth as ends all strife;
> Such a life as killeth death.
>
> Come, my Light, my Feast, my Strength;
> Such a light as shows a feast;
> Such a feast as mends in length;
> Such a strength as makes his guest.
>
> Come, my Joy, my Love, my Heart;
> Such a joy as none can move;
> Such a love as none can part;
> Such a heart as joys in love.

According to the *Hymnal Companion*, the phrase "such a feast as mends in length" means that the feast only gets better as it continues.

Can participants come up with some of their own?

"The greatest single distinguishing feature of the omnipotence of God is that our imagination gets lost when thinking about it."

Blaise Pascal, *Pensees*, I, XV

Describing a Mystery

Find in the Bible the passage you chose and complete your section or sections of the chart below. Write the metaphor or word image in the chart, and write what you think this comparison tells us about God.

Report to the whole group. Complete the same chart on the board or newsprint as each image is reported.

Bible Passage	Simile/Metaphor	Reveals What About God?
Example: Psalm 23	**Shepherd, gracious host**	**Comforts; provides; generous**
Luke 15:8-10		
Luke 15:11-24		
Psalm 31:3		
Psalm 3:3		
Matthew 20:1-16		
Luke 14:15-24		
John 15:1-2		
Psalm 27:1		
Psalm 90:1		
Deut. 32:11-12		
Revelation 21:6		

Permission is granted to photocopy this handout for use with this session.

>>> **SESSION 5**

GOD IS TRINITY >>>

>>> KEY VERSE

In the beginning was the Word, and the Word was with God, and the Word was God. (John 1:1)

>>> FAITH STORY

John 1:1-8; John 14:25-26; Matthew 28:18-20

>>> FAITH FOCUS

John said that the Jesus who entered historic time was also the Word who was with God in the beginning at the creation. In Matthew, Jesus told the disciples to baptize in the name of the Father, Son, and Holy Spirit. Considering these scriptures, the early church councils created a doctrine that said God is a tri-unity: three-in-one and one-in-three. God is Creator, Word, and Spirit; but above all, God is a mystery beyond our complete comprehension.

>>> SESSION GOAL

Empower participants to wrestle with the mystery of God's being as three-in-one and one-in-three, and to see how each part of the Trinity expands their understanding of God.

TEACHING PLAN

1. FOCUS 10-15 minutes

>>> **Option A:** Distribute copies of the handout sheet and writing utensils. Give participants 5-8 minutes to figure out the relationship puzzles, then go over the answers.

Answers:

1. She would be your great-grandmother.
2. He would be your nephew.
3. She would be your stepmother.
4. That would be you.
5. She would be your first cousin.
6. She would be your great-aunt.
7. She would be your niece.
8. He would be your grandfather.

(Adapted from *The Cokesbury Game Book*, Arthur M. Depew)

Go to **Option A**, Connect.

>>> Materials needed and advance preparation

- Copies of the handout sheet and pencils or pens (*Option A*, Focus)
- Invite a parishioner to come to your meeting well disguised (*Option B*, Focus).
- Tasks written on slips of paper; basket or hat (*Option C*, Focus)
- Slips of paper and pencils (*Option B*, Connect)
- Bibles
- Prepare mini-lecture on Trinity (see Insights and Explore)
- A glass of water, a cup of ice, and a thermos full of very hot water (see choice in Explore)
- Song books (*Option C*, Respond)

>> **Option B:** Have a member of the parish come in well disguised and stand or sit in front of the group. Invite the participants to try to guess who the mystery person is by playing Twenty Questions. Up to 20 questions may be asked, but only questions that can be answered yes or no.

Variation: Instead of disguising someone, simply tell participants you're thinking of a certain person in the parish, and have them guess the identity by asking you the 20 questions.

Go to **Option B**, Connect.

>> **Option C:** Write the following tasks on slips of paper (and add your own that fit well with your own group). Have participants pair up, draw a task out of a hat or basket, and perform the task, which would be simple were it not for the conditions!

- Write several sentences with the hand you do not normally write with.
- Communicate to your partner what you did yesterday without speaking or writing.
- Move to the opposite side of the room without using your legs.
- Decide where to go out to lunch without talking or looking at each other.

Allow 5-7 minutes to choose a solution and accomplish the task. When everyone is finished, ask each pair to share what their task was and how they carried it out. Then have a group vote on which pair had the most difficult task. Go to **Option C**, Connect.

2. CONNECT 5-10 minutes

>> **Option A:** Ask the participants: *How many of you like puzzles, riddles, and mysteries? What do you like or dislike about them? How do you feel when you figure them out? How about when you cannot solve one?*

>> **Option B:** Ask: *How difficult was it to guess the mystery guest? What would it have been like if I had asked the mystery guest to leave without your knowing who it was (or if you had gotten to 20 questions without guessing the identity and we stopped the game)? What would have made it easier to guess who the mystery guest was?*

One thing that makes it easier to discover someone's identity is when they reveal something about themselves. Play "Who's Who?" by giving each person a slip of paper and inviting them to **list 5 names** that apply to them because of things they do. Examples might be: student, musician, soccer player, baby sitter, son, sister. Have the group exchange cards and guess which card identifies which person.

>> **Option C:** Ask participants what made these tasks difficult. Then ask them to name some other difficult things they've been asked to do. Give examples if participants get stuck.

3. EXPLORE THE BIBLE 10-15 minutes

Shift to this activity by saying: *The Bible presents us with puzzles or mysteries that are difficult to understand or figure out concerning who God is. Listen to this one:*

Read to the participants John 1:1-3. Ask the participants: *What can we know about God from this passage? What can we find out about the Word? What is the relationship between the two?* What makes this passage puzzling and difficult is partly that human beings try to think in terms of substance and physical being.

Then read John 14:25-26. Ask: *What can we know about God from this passage? What is the Holy Spirit's relationship to God and Word?*

Note: Participants may have heard various references to the Trinity and to the parts of the Trinity referred to as "persons." It is challenging to define the three unique persons in the One. Be patient and ready to help as they puzzle it out.

Give a *brief* mini-lecture covering the material in Insights from Scripture on the early church arguments over the doctrine of the Trinity. Explain that the word Trinity is not found in the Bible; it is a doctrine of the church. The idea of God as three is found in the Bible in the sense that God is named as acting in three major ways: as Creator/God (Genesis 1; John 1), Jesus/Word (Mark 1; John 1), and as Holy Spirit (Genesis 1; Romans 8; John 14).

The full meaning of saying that God is three-in-one cannot be known. It remains a mystery. Perhaps one of the best ways to illustrate what three-in-one might mean is to show or simply tell about **water**. Point out the liquid water, ice, and hot water (steaming in the thermos). The liquid people drink, the ice they put in their cups and glasses, and the steam from a sauna or a boiling pot are all of the same *substance* (H_2O). But they are *in form* three distinct things. *Another analogy:* Remind participants how one person can be a mother, a sister, and a daughter, but remain one and the same person.

4. APPLY 15-20 minutes

Form pairs. Distribute song books and have participants find songs about the "persons" of the Trinity. Have them write a "Who's Who" biographical paragraph or create a commercial advertising each "person" of the Trinity. Allow 10-12 minutes to work and then have the pairs read their biographical entry to the group or present their commercial.

5. RESPOND 5-10 minutes

》》 Option A: Invite participants to close their eyes and visualize the following. *Who would you call on...*

- *if you were lonely?*
- *if you needed money?*
- *if you ran out of gas?*
- *if you had a serious problem?*
- *if you needed a good laugh and wanted to have some fun?*

Point out that no one person can meet all the needs another person has. That is why people have a number of friends and family members, all of whom are an important part of their lives. The persons of the Trinity can meet different needs in different situations. Invite the participants to continue visualizing. *When would you call on…*

- *God the Creator?*
- *Jesus Christ?*
- *the Holy Spirit?*

》》 Option B: Write a personal letter to one person of the Trinity sharing your thoughts/feelings about anything in your life at this time and what you would like from God. Distribute writing materials (or use the back of the handout). Allow 5 minutes for writing. Then close with prayer.

》》 Option C: Sing a song about the Trinity or one person of the Trinity. Close with a prayer that addresses all three persons of the Trinity, such as a doxology.

》》 LOOK AHEAD

If you plan to use the Extender Session, contact participants or tell them at the end of this session to bring in music that speaks of God.

INSIGHTS FROM SCRIPTURE

The word *Trinity* is not found in the Bible. The trinity is a doctrine of the church. Most of the New Testament, except for some of Paul's letters, is not particularly concerned about doctrines and theology. It is concerned with the good news of Jesus and the ministry of the newly formed church.

The idea of God as three *is* found in the Bible in the sense that God is named as acting in three major ways: as Creator/God (Genesis 1; John 1), Jesus/Word (Mark 1; John 1), and as Holy Spirit (Genesis 1; Romans 8; John 14). The unity of the three "persons" of God is suggested as they are named together in the baptismal formula given by Jesus on the mountain (Matthew 28:19) and in an epistle blessing (2 Corinthians 13:13). These references and others prompted the church to create the doctrine of the trinitarian formula.

HISTORICAL CONTROVERSY

Creation of doctrine is not a simple thing, however. The idea of Trinity came about little by little during a time when controversy about heretical beliefs was strong in the church.

During the first century of the emerging church, Christians understood God as Creator. Some of them had even seen Jesus, God's Son. Some had experienced the coming of the Holy Spirit, whom Jesus had promised would be sent to the disciples after he ascended to God. In the later first and second centuries, while the Christian church was very young, people argued over just how to understand God's being.

A scholar named Justin Martyr proclaimed Christ to be another God. In the second century, Marcion declared that the God described in the ancient Hebrew writings and the one of the New Testament was not the same. A group called the Gnostics (Greek, *gnosis* = knowledge) claimed that Jesus was a heavenly messenger, who only *seemed* to have an earthly body, almost like a ghost. Others argued that Jesus was a really exceptional human being who was "adopted" by God. Monarchians argued that God was only a single person, and that the Son and the Holy Spirit were merely other "modes" of God's being.

A man named Tertullian chimed in by writing and speaking of God as three persons and *at the same time* a unity. Controversy continued, and in 325 C.E. a great council was held at Nicaea in Asia Minor. Many bishops signed a confession that affirmed that God was Father/Creator, Son/Jesus Christ, and Holy Spirit. Three-in-One, and One-in-three.

For 50 more years, arguments continued. Eusebius argued that the Holy Spirit was less than, or subordinate to God and Jesus. Finally, three church leaders who came to be known as the Three Cappadocians (Basil the Great, Gregory of Nyssa, and Gregory of Nazianzus) said that Father/Creator, Son/Jesus Christ, and Holy Spirit were all of one substance or essence, with three special forms or persons. Another council was held in 381 C.E., at which time this belief was put in writing.

> "The Christian community, though with all its human limitations, can become a reflection of the communion of the Trinity, of its goodness and beauty."
>
> Pope Francis

» DRY DOCTRINE

People today don't have time or patience for doctrine or absolutes that have little to do with their daily lives. Sharing part of the historic struggle, and inviting participants to explore how the idea of the "three persons," or divine ways of acting expands their notion of God might make the session more practical and interesting.

Because the idea of Trinity was formalized out of conflict against heretical beliefs about God, Trinity in some ways tells us more about what God is *not* than what God is. Our concept of who God is will be diminished if we focus on trying to keep out heretics, or if we insist on thinking of God in terms of substance and matter. Believers should be careful not to limit God by boxing the Divine into human categories of knowledge.

Getting to know you

In Real Life — Exploring tough questions facing youth today

1. What would be your relation to your aunt's mother's father's wife?
2. What would be your relation to your sister-in-law's father-in-law's grandson?
3. What would be your relation to your sister's father's stepson's mother?
4. What would be your relation to your uncle's father's grandchild?
5. What would be your relation to your father's father's daughter's daughter?
6. What would be your relation to your father's uncle's brother's sister?
7. What would be your relation to the granddaughter of the only son of your mother's mother-in-law?
8. What would be your relation to your brother-in-law's wife's grandmother's husband?

Permission is granted to photocopy this handout for use with this session.

>>> EXTENDER SESSION
(best used after Session 5)

GOD IN MUSIC/ WAYS OF KNOWING

>> SESSION GOAL
Discuss and evaluate what musicians have expressed about God.

>> SESSION PLAN
Invite participants to bring samples of music that speak about God. Listen to some of each. **Compare and contrast the views of God** presented there. Bring music yourself as a stimulus or back-up.

Next, group brainstorm **all the ways we know things**. Prime the pump by mentioning a few of these:

- trusting the word of another person (ask someone, interview an expert, read a book)
- observation
- hearing
- intuition
- tradition
- laws or legal precedent
- personal experience
- logical deduction or proof
- faith
- fiction or stories
- experiment
- theory
- the Bible
- repeatability

Go back and listen again to music that was brought and...

  A. Evaluate songs or phrases according to the ways of knowing the group listed. *What music uses repetition to help reinforce an idea? What music points to tradition as a way we learn of God? What music tells a story with a lesson to be learned? Is any of the music about the Bible?* Continue in this fashion...

  B. Ask people what music they remember from when they were younger and what messages they carry with them because of it. *Is there a particular piece of music or song that goes straight to your heart?* Note how music and lyrics help pass on the ways we know about God and the human experience of life. Sometimes, it helps us express a way of knowing God that is not able to be expressed any other way.

>> Materials needed and advance preparation

- Contact participants prior to the session and ask them to bring music that speaks to them of God, in lyrics or not. Bring music yourself as stimulus or back-up.
- Music/media player
- Chalkboard/chalk or newsprint/markers

In Real Life
Exploring tough questions facing youth today

CLUELESS AND CALLED
Discipleship and the Gospel of Mark

What does it take to be a disciple? This study of the Gospel of Mark focuses on the requirements for following Jesus' way and the abundant life that is ours as a result. (5 sessions)

DO MIRACLES HAPPEN?
Signs and Wonders in the Gospel of John

The greatest miracle, recorded in John 1:14 and 3:16, is the miracle of God's love that became flesh and lived among us. But John also included examples of what we more traditionally think of as miracles: the wonder of abundance from little; healing; signs of impossibility and faith; and the resurrection. (5 sessions)

DO THE RIGHT THING
Ethics Shaped by Faith

How do you know what's right and what's wrong? Even when you figure it out, the right thing is often the unpopular or unpleasant choice. This unit offers participants a clearer sense of what it means to claim a faith identity, a foundation that can help them sort out the gritty details of ethics shaped by faith. (6 sessions)

FIGHT RIGHT
A Christian Approach to Conflict Resolution

This unit will help youth understand conflict and its function. They will learn how they can be honest and loving, and explore how conflict can be used for positive results. They will also learn ways to enhance their communication skills. 1 Corinthians. (5 sessions)

GOD IS A WARRIOR?
Violence in the Bible

The Bible challenges us to be reconciled to one another and work for justice. So what do we do with the stories that seem to condone violence or even encourage it? A discussion of issues in the Old and New Testaments. (6 sessions)

HOW DO YOU KNOW?
Wisdom in the Bible

Wisdom literature teaches us that we gain knowledge of the world, ourselves, and God through experience and observation. This unit provides practical, hands-on wisdom to help young people avoid life's snares and grow closer to God. Proverbs, Job, Ecclesiastes. (5 sessions)

HOW TO BE A TRUE FRIEND
The Bible Reveals Friendship's Heart

To be a friend takes skill. Help youth discover the secrets of friendship through various stories from the Old and New Testament. (6 sessions)

HOW TO READ THE BIBLE
Building Skills for Bible Study

What kind of book is the Bible? What does this book mean to me? This unit looks at the Bible as revelation, as history, as literature. Selected scripture. (5 sessions)

KEEPING THE GARDEN
A Faith Response to God's Creation

If Christians believe that God made the world, we do not need any more compelling reason to care for it than that God has handed us a treasure to hold and protect. This unit gets beyond trendy environmentalism and challenges youth to see environmental awareness as a religious issue. Genesis. (6 sessions)

MANTRAS, MENORAHS, AND MINARETS
Encountering Other Faiths

How is Christianity different from other faiths? Why do others believe the way they do? This study can give youth a new appreciation for the uniqueness of Jesus. Selected scripture. (5 sessions)

SALT, LIGHT, AND THE GOOD LIFE
The Beatitudes and the Sermon on the Mount

What can youth expect in a life of discipleship? This unit explores the Sermon on the Mount under four main sections: the Beatitudes, Salt and Light, Jesus and the Law, and Heavenly Teachings. Matthew 5. (6 sessions)

A SPECK IN THE UNIVERSE
The Bible on Self-Esteem and Peer Pressure

Discover God's unconditional love and acceptance of all people. This study will show positive ways to have one's life make a difference, and help youth find ways to resist negative peer pressure and turn it into positive action. (6 sessions)

THE RADICAL REIGN
Parables of Jesus

Jesus used parables to reveal what the kingdom of God is like, and how God relates to us. This study highlights how the parables reveal God's reign as radically different from the world we live in, and what that means for the Christian life. (6 sessions)

TESTING THE WATERS
Basic Tenets of Faith

Discover the biblical roots for the central Christian concepts of covenant, community, and baptism. This short course is a way to test the (baptismal) waters of Christianity before diving in, or review the basics for those who already have. (6 sessions)

WHO IS GOD?
Engaging the Mystery

God is beyond human comprehension, yet desires to be known. These sessions focus on the way we get clues about and glimpses of God from the Bible, God's creation, and church tradition. Selected scripture. (5 sessions)

www.ingramcontent.com/pod-product-compliance
Lightning Source LLC
Chambersburg PA
CBHW080326170426
43193CB00030B/2862